# FROGS PLAY CELLOS

## and other fun facts

For my new friend, Elliot
—**L. D.**

For S&S
—**H. E.**

To Lydia and Jackie
—**A. S.**

To Allison
—**P. O.**

LITTLE SIMON
An imprint of Simon & Schuster Children's Publishing Division
1230 Avenue of the Americas, New York, New York 10020
This Little Simon edition October 2014
Series concept by Laura Lyn DiSiena
Copyright © 2014 by Simon & Schuster, Inc.
All rights reserved, including the right of reproduction in whole or in part in any form.
LITTLE SIMON is a registered trademark of Simon & Schuster, Inc., and associated colophon is a trademark of Simon & Schuster, Inc.
For information about special discounts for bulk purchases, please contact Simon & Schuster Special Sales at 1-866-506-1949
or business@simonandschuster.com. The Simon & Schuster Speakers Bureau can bring authors to your live event. For more information
or to book an event contact the Simon & Schuster Speakers Bureau at 1-866-248-3049 or visit our website at www.simonspeakers.com.
Designed by Ciara Gay.
Manufactured in China 0714 SCP
10 9 8 7 6 5 4 3 2 1
This book has been cataloged with the Library of Congress.
ISBN 978-1-4814-1425-8 (pbk)
ISBN 978-1-4814-1426-5 (hc)
ISBN 978-1-4814-1427-2 (eBook)

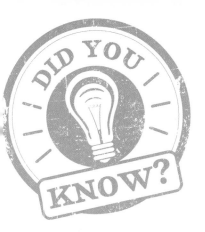
# FROGS PLAY CELLOS

## and other fun facts

By Laura Lyn DiSiena and Hannah Eliot
Illustrated by Pete Oswald and Aaron Spurgeon

LITTLE SIMON
New York  London  Toronto  Sydney  New Delhi

DO-RE-MI-FA-SO-LA~

Oh, hello! Do you like music? Do you know how to play any instruments? How about the didgeridoo? That's an Australian wind instrument.

What about the cello? Did you know that the cello is so big and heavy that cellists have to sit down to play it? How about that the cello section of an orchestra is always stage left, which means it's on the *right* when you're looking at the stage from the audience? Or that when a cello's string is plucked, it vibrates and moves the air around it, producing sound waves? Okay, okay. Maybe you knew those things. But did you know that FROGS play cellos?

You see, in order to play a cello, you need a bow. And every bow has what's called a "frog." This is the part of the bow you hold when you play a string instrument. Along with being the handle, the frog clamps the bow hairs at this end. It has a metal piece that you twist to tighten and loosen the strings in order to adjust the sound of the instrument.

RiBBiT! RiBBiT!

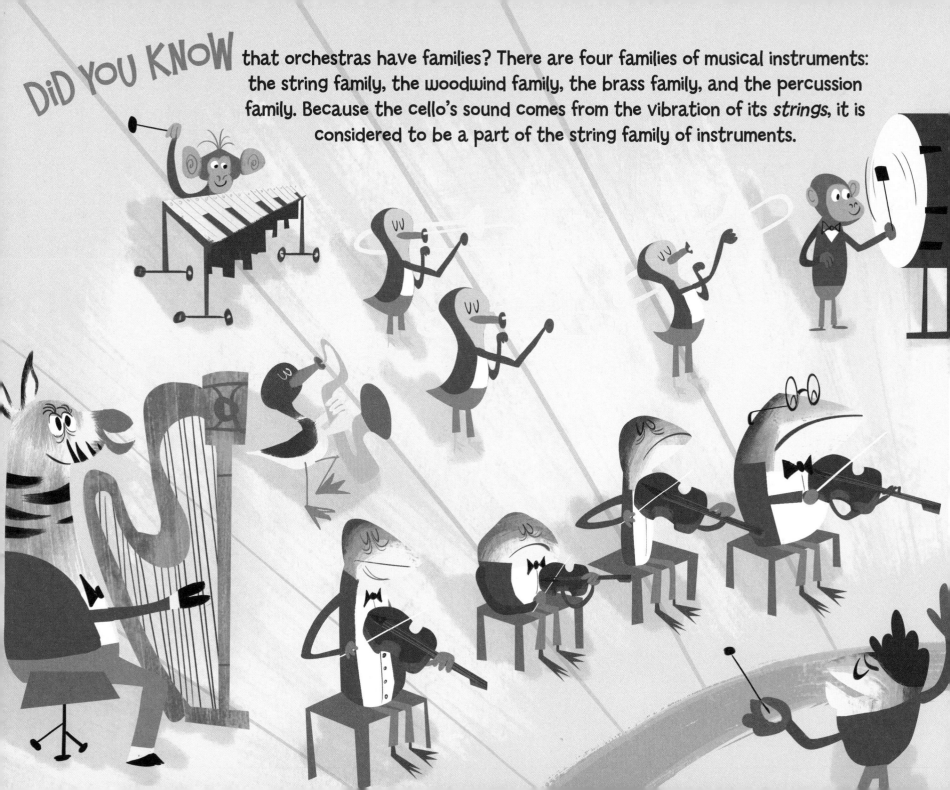

**DID YOU KNOW** that orchestras have families? There are four families of musical instruments: the string family, the woodwind family, the brass family, and the percussion family. Because the cello's sound comes from the vibration of its *strings*, it is considered to be a part of the string family of instruments.

Do you know what instrument in the orchestra has the most strings? The piano!
The average piano has about 230 strings, and just like the cello, a pianist needs to sit in
order to play it. When a pianist plays a key, a hammer inside the piano lifts and strikes a
string. This is what makes the sound. The piano has the largest range of any instrument
in the orchestra, and is unique because you can play many notes at once!

So with ALL those strings playing ALL those notes,
what family do you think the piano is a part of?
If you guessed string, you'd be right. But the piano
is ALSO a member of the percussion family— CRASH! BANG!

Oh, don't be frightened. Those are just other percussion instruments. These instruments make their sounds by being hit, shaken, or banged. Sounds like fun, doesn't it? Cymbals, two metal discs that are banged together, are the noisiest of the whole orchestra. Modern cymbals are untuned so they don't play different notes, but they sure do add excitement to the music!

Wait a second—are you still wondering how the piano is part of the percussion family? Well, it's because the hammers inside a piano *hit* the strings, just as you would *hit* two cymbals together!

Have you ever played a xylophone? Wow, that sure is a tricky word.
Let's say it again. Here's a hint: the "x" sounds like a "z."
XY-LO-PHONE

If you've played the xylophone, you know that you hit the keys with
a special type of hammer called a mallet. Using a mallet, you can
make different bright notes that sound kind of like bells.

We aren't entirely sure where the xylophone came from, but we think it was developed in Southeast Asia around the year 800 and then came to Africa.

Normally you think of hammers and mallets as construction tools. For example, if you're building a top-secret superpowered tree house, you'd probably need a hammer to construct it.

Did you know that there are lots of *other* tools and everyday objects often used in music? Can you name any? How about one you'd find in your own kitchen? It's the spoon! That's right, folk music from all over the world uses spoons in a variety of ways for entertainment.

In Greek folk music, dancers use beautifully decorated wooden spoons to make a beat for their dance rhythms.

In Russia the spoons not only make an appearance in folk music, but sometimes in actual orchestras!

American folk music uses metal spoons and other objects, such as jugs and washboards. When all of these things are played together, they create a *very* unique type of harmony!

Speaking of different cultures, let's talk about Native American music. Drums are a very important part of the Native American culture. These instruments keep the rhythm steady for singers and dancers as they perform.

But music isn't only for fun in the Native American community. Often the singers and dancers are telling stories as they perform, as well as passing on customs and history from one generation to the next.

Drums are used in all types of music. Musicians use drums of different sizes, materials, and sounds depending on the type of music they are playing. For example, a jazz musician might want a drum that's high-pitched and quiet, whereas a rock musician might want a drum that's low-pitched and loud.

# ROCK AND ROLL, BABY!

Rock and roll was created in America in the 1950s when parts of country music, blues, gospel, and jazz all merged together. Besides drums, a rock band typically also has at least one electric guitar, a bass guitar, and a singer. Do you have a favorite rock and roll band?

The Rock and Roll Hall of Fame is in Cleveland, Ohio. Did you know that John Lennon, one of the founding members of the Beatles, was inducted into the Hall of Fame *twice*? Even though the Beatles no longer exists as a group, it is still the bestselling band of *all time* in the United States.

Opera is another type of musical performance. But opera has been around since *long* before rock concerts! It was created during the Renaissance when a group of artists, musicians, and poets got together and figured out a way to make the ancient Greek plays of the past popular again. Opera is a play where all the spoken parts are sung!

LA, LA, LA!

LA, LA, LA!

Have you heard of Beethoven? Born in 1770, he was—and still is—one of the most famous composers ever. A composer is someone who creates music. Beethoven only wrote 1 opera, but he *did* compose 9 symphonies, 7 concertos, 17 string quartets, 32 piano sonatas, 10 violin sonatas, 5 cello sonatas, and a sonata for the French horn.

The clarinet is an orchestra instrument that is often played during operas. What family do you think the clarinet is in? The woodwinds! The clarinet is a wooden instrument that makes its sound when a musician blows air into it. Even though *all* woodwinds were originally made of wood, today some are made of metal. The flute, for example, is now made of silver, gold, or platinum. FANCY!

The theremin is an electronic instrument that was patented in the 1920s. It is used in various kinds of music, but it is especially known for being used in early horror films. Because of this, it is associated with a very eerie sound. SPOOKY!

A film score is original music written for a movie. Movies were first shown in theaters in the early 1900's, but there was no *sound* in them—they were silent! So usually an in-house pianist or organist would play music to accompany the film. These days, music is incorporated into the film. But do you want to know something funny? Many film scores use advanced digital technology so it *sounds* like there's live music playing!

Speaking of live music, the brass family of instruments can play louder than any other in the orchestra. Can you think of an instrument in the brass family? The tuba? How about the trumpet?
Did you know that the trumpet is one of the oldest instruments in existence?

In fact, the first trumpets ever used were made of conch shells!

The harmonica is an instrument that's much smaller than the trumpet. The harmonica is also pretty easy to play. You can make lots of different sounds just by inhaling and then exhaling into the side that has evenly spaced channels. To make things even easier than that, you can wear a harmonica holder on your shoulders. The holder loops around and clamps the harmonica in front of your mouth . . . so you can play with no hands!

Why would someone want to play the harmonica without using their hands?

Well, what if their hands were busy playing another instrument, like the accordion?
And what if they also had cymbals strapped between their knees? SMASH!
And a drum on their back with a foot pedal connected to the beater! BOOM! BOOM!
And don't forget the tambourines tied to their arms. SHAKE! SHAKE!

Now that's a one-man band! A one-man band is a musician that plays all different kinds of instruments at once. Some musicians even use electric drum pads, keyboards, and guitars.
One-man bands have existed since the 13th century, and different types of them can still be seen performing all over the world.

Something that's also existed for a long time—since the creation of the world, actually—is animal music. Whales, birds, and other animals are thought to make their own kind of music. Scientists have noted that birds' songs even follow specific rhythms, patterns, and pitches that are similar to what we find in music composed by human musicians!

Birds may be able to sing beautifully, but unlike frogs, they certainly can't PLAY THE CELLO!

# MORE FUN FACTS

**Piano:** Some nicknames for piano-playing, or the piano itself, are "tickling the ivories," "the black and whites," and "the eighty-eight."

**Cymbal:** The size of the cymbal affects its sound. Usually, the larger the cymbal, the louder and *longer* the sound.

**Cello:** Though the cello is huge, it's not the biggest string instrument in the modern orchestra. The double bass is!

**Flute:** The hyperbass flute is pitched so low that it's outside what scientists consider the range of human hearing!

**Folk music:** Scottish folk music uses bagpipes!

**Opera:** In the 17th century, women were not allowed to sing on stage. So men with really high voices had t perform the female role

**Film score:** The American Film Institute considers *Star Wars* to be the top film score of all time.

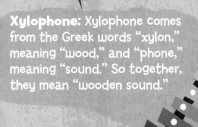

**Xylophone:** Xylophone comes from the Greek words "xylon," meaning "wood," and "phone," meaning "sound." So together, they mean "wooden sound."

**Rock-and-roll:** The "British Invasion" occurred in the mid-1960s when rock and pop music acts from the United Kingdom—bands such as the Beatles, the Rolling Stones, and the Who—became popular in the United States . . . and then throughout the world.

**Drums:** Rattle drums contain little pellets within the shell, or have knotted cords attached to the drum, and are played by being shaken.

**Harmonica:** Playing the harmonica is actually good exercise for your lungs!

**Trumpet:** Many jazz trumpet players use a technique called growling. They simultaneously hum while playing a note, which creates two sets of vibrations that interfere with each other and create a growling sound!

**Animal music:** Two types of whales are known to produce whale songs—the humpback whale and a subspecies of the blue whale.

**One-man band:** A loop pedal records and then repeats a short piece of music so that one-man bands can play over the repeated loop.

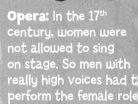